NoLex 11/12

Anthony
Mason

by Mark Stewart

ACKNOWLEDGMENTS

The editors wish to thank Anthony Mason for his cooperation in preparing this book.
Thanks also to Integrated Sports International for their assistance.

PHOTO CREDITS

All photos courtesy AP/Wide World Photos, Inc. except the following:

Vince Manniello/Sports Chrome – Cover, 5 top, 6, 8
Louis Raynor/Sports Chrome – 46 left
Tennessee State University – 15, 20 bottom left
Mark Stewart – 48

STAFF

Project Coordinator: John Sammis, Cronopio Publishing
Series Design Concept: The Sloan Group
Design and Electronic Page Makeup: Jaffe Enterprises, and
    Digital Communications Services, Inc.

LIBRARY OF CONGRESS CATALOGING-IN-PUBLICATION DATA

Stewart, Mark.
    Anthony Mason / by Mark Stewart.
      p. cm. – (Grolier all-pro biographies)
    Includes index.
    Summary: A brief biography of New York Knicks player Anthony Mason.
    ISBN 0-516-20138-7 (lib. binding) – 0-516-26000-6 (pbk.)
    1. Mason, Anthony, 1963-   –Juvenile literature. 2. Basketball players–United States–
Biography–Juvenile literature. (1. Mason, Anthony, 1963- . 2. Basketball players.)
I. Title. II. Series.
GV884.M35S84 1996
796.323'092–dc20
(B)   96-5104
                                                                                              CIP
                                                                                              AC

Grolier **ALL-PRO** *Biographies*™

Anthony Mason

by
Mark Stewart

CHILDREN'S PRESS®
A Division of Grolier Publishing
New York • London • Hong Kong • Sydney
Danbury, Connecticut

Contents

Who

Am I?

Someone once said that basketball players are born, not made. Well, I am living proof that this is not true. Not too long ago, there was not a single team that wanted me. People said I was clumsy and that I could not shoot well enough to make it as a pro. But playing in the NBA was my dream, so I decided to do whatever I had to do—and go wherever I had to go—to develop into a solid, all-around basketball player. My name is Anthony Mason, and this is my story ... "

"I decided to do whatever I had to do . . . to develop into a solid, all-around basketball player."

Growing Up

When Anthony Mason was seven years old, his mother bought him his first basketball. It was not as important a day as you might think, considering that he turned out to be a basketball star. At that time in his life, Anthony was more interested in baseball! He rooted for the New York Yankees, and one of his favorite players was Chris Chambliss, the team's first baseman.

Anthony grew up with his two brothers and his mother, Mary. His father did not live with the family. For a time, Mary Mason was a

switchboard operator. Later, she became a bookkeeper, which required her to keep track of how much money her company made and how much it spent.

Anthony worked hard and did very well in school. One of his first teachers, Ms. Drew, made a big impression on Anthony because she always seemed to be able to bring out the best in her class. Ms. Drew really cared about Anthony and his friends. She helped them to believe in themselves.

Anthony's favorite subjects were social studies and science. He liked social studies because it gave him a chance to discover interesting things about people in other parts of the world. He could also learn what it was like to live at different times in history. This made him more aware of his own surroundings and helped him to appreciate the advantages of living in a big city like New York. Science interested Anthony because he liked to understand what makes things work. He especially enjoyed learning about the muscles, bones, and senses of the human body.

After years of growing up with baseball as his number-one sport, Anthony fell in love with basketball in 1979, the year that college stars Magic Johnson and Larry Bird met in the NCAA championship game. Like millions of kids across the country, Anthony watched with excitement as these amazing players made the game look easy and fun. A year later, the Mason family moved from Passaic, New Jersey, to Queens, New York. They settled into the community of Springfield Gardens. In Anthony's new neighborhood, all of the kids played basketball, so he decided to visit the local courts. At 14, he was very big for his age—over six feet tall. Anthony thought his

Larry Bird grabs a loose ball from Magic Johnson during the 1979 NCAA championship game.

"Dr. J" Julius Erving

height would give him an advantage against the other players, but he was wrong. Anthony lacked many of the basic skills that the shorter players had already learned, such as dribbling, passing, and shooting. So he spent a lot of time at the playground, practicing for hours at a time. Slowly but surely, his game began to improve.

When he was a teenager, Anthony got his first job packing clothing for a company on 36th Street in New York City. On 33rd Street was Madison Square Garden, home of the New York Knicks. Anthony dreamed that, someday, he would be playing basketball in front of 19,000 cheering fans . . . just three blocks away! Even though Anthony lived in New York and followed the Knicks, his basketball hero was a Philadelphia 76er, the legendary "Dr. J," Julius Erving. "Dr. J. grew up just a few miles from where I lived in Queens. I loved his incredible leaping ability and slam dunks, but I also admired him for being a team leader who helped make the other players around him better."

As he entered Springfield Gardens High School, Anthony was still pursuing baseball more than basketball. His nickname was "Goose," after Goose Gossage, the star pitcher of the New York Yankees.

In his third year of high school, Anthony met Ken Fiedler, the Springfield Gardens basketball coach. Coach Fiedler saw something he liked in the young man. He put Anthony on the basketball team as a substitute player and worked closely with him during and after the season. Anthony became the team's star in his senior season, and his school won the city championship.

After joining the basketball team, Anthony had time for little else besides basketball practice and schoolwork. Anthony worked hard to keep up in the classroom, and he maintained a B+ average. When he spent an evening at home reading for

Anthony's teammates nicknamed him "Goose," after New York Yankees pitcher Goose Gossage.

homework assignments, Anthony thought it was fun and interesting. "I was very lucky. Reading was not as difficult for me as it was for some of my friends. Still, it took a lot of practice before I became good at it—kind of like what happened to me in basketball! I realize now how important reading is. It helps give you the wisdom to think things through. It also helps you to connect with the world around you, and enables you to discover new things about yourself. For example, when I read *Native Son*, a novel by Richard Wright, I learned some important things about overcoming challenges. It helped me understand who I am, where I come from, and what I can be. The bottom line is that you cannot function if you cannot read. It is a part of survival."

Anthony's hard work in school and in basketball practice paid off when he finally made it to the NBA.

College

Anthony's good grades and his basketball talent earned him a basketball scholarship to Tennessee State University. When Anthony Mason went to college, he was scared. It would be the first time he had been away from home, except for a summer he spent at Coach Fiedler's basketball camp. Fiedler, who had worked hard to get Anthony a scholarship, told him not to worry. He was never more than a phone call away. Anthony did not tell his coach at the time, but he considered him the father he never had. In fact, when he was filling out the forms to register for classes at Tennessee State, in the space asking for his father's name, Anthony wrote "Ken Fiedler."

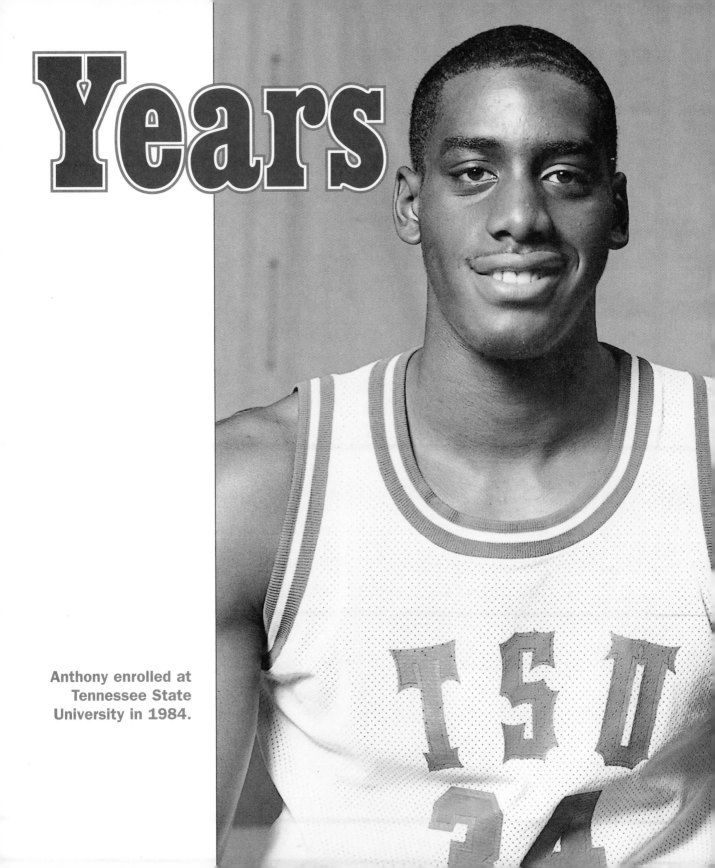

Years

Anthony enrolled at Tennessee State University in 1984.

Anthony continued working hard both on and off the basketball court when he got to college. He studied criminal justice, a subject that usually leads to a career in law or law enforcement. Meanwhile, he became one of the basketball team's top players. Prior to his senior season, Anthony added 40 pounds of muscle to his already massive body and had a great year. He played every position on the court—including point guard!—and averaged an astounding 28.0 points per game. This figure was the third-best in the country. For the first time Anthony Mason was noticed by scouts for NBA teams.

Tennessee State had produced two other basketball stars before Anthony Mason: Dick Barnett, starting guard on the first New York Knicks NBA championship team in 1970, and Leonard "Truck" Robinson, who led the NBA in rebounding during the 1977–78 season.

Anthony's college stats show how he improved each year:

REBOUNDS PER GAME

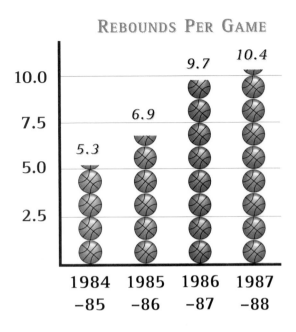

5.3	6.9	9.7	10.4

10.0
7.5
5.0
2.5

1984	1985	1986	1987
−85	−86	−87	−88

POINTS PER GAME

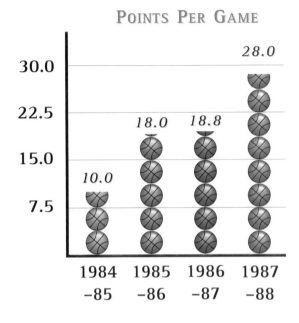

10.0	18.0	18.8	28.0

30.0
22.5
15.0
7.5

1984	1985	1986	1987
−85	−86	−87	−88

Tennessee State graduates Dick Barnett (left) and Leonard "Truck" Robinson (right)

17

Road to

Because Anthony Mason did not play for a famous college team, many scouts believed his great statistics were misleading. They claimed, for instance, that a legitimate scorer should be a better outside shooter than Anthony.

They failed to see that Anthony had scored his points using the other skills he had developed, such as quickness, strength, and ball-handling ability. Anthony knew that if someone gave him the chance to play and learn in the NBA, he might improve his shooting and become a star. Unfortunately for Anthony, no one saw it this way. He was not selected until the end of the college draft by the Portland Trail Blazers, who told him he probably would not make the team. So began one of the most remarkable journeys in basketball history.

Anthony set off on a search for a pro team that would give him a lot of playing time. His first stop was Turkey, where he worked out with weights, practiced, and played basketball virtually all day. It was a brutal schedule. Anthony would run

the Pros

up and down the hills around the city wearing a 50-pound vest. He also played one-on-one games that did not stop for fouls . . . and did not end until one player reached 200 baskets!

Poor Anthony got so homesick that his mother had to quit her job and fly over to Turkey to keep him company. But when he finally returned to the United States, he was ready to take on anyone in basketball!

"Over the next two seasons I played for the New Jersey Nets and the Denver Nuggets, but I was usually one of the last men to get in the game. I also played in the Continental Basketball Association (CBA) for the Tulsa Fast Breakers, and I averaged 29.9 points and 14.8 rebounds a game. That summer, while playing for the Long Island Surf in the United States Basketball League, I caught the eye of the New York Knicks and was invited to try out for the team. The coaching staff liked what they saw, and I made it! All those years I just worked hard and kept the faith that God would pull me through. And He did."

Timeline

1981: Gets his first job, across from Madison Square Garden

1991: Joins the New York Knicks and plays in all 82 games

1984: Leaves home in Queens, New York, to attend Tennessee State University

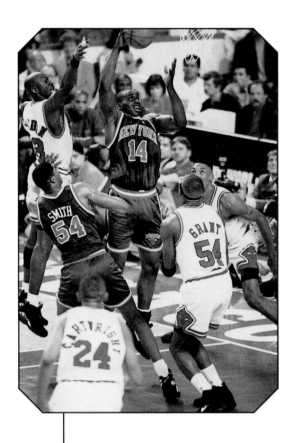

1995: Wins NBA Sixth Man award

1993: Leads the Knicks to the NBA Eastern Conference championship

1994: Knicks come within one game of the NBA title

21

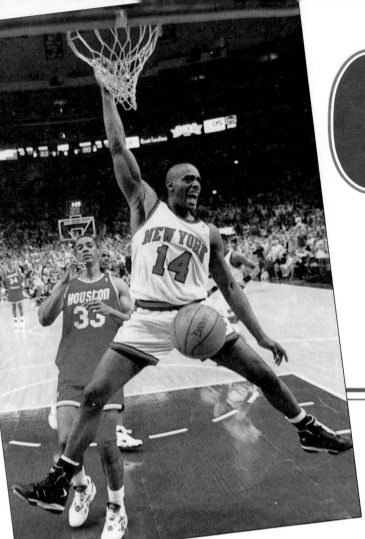

Game

Anthony delivers a
spectacular slam dunk.

Smaller players have a hard time preventing me from
establishing position close to the basket. For most of the
league's big men, I am too quick to cover on the open floor. On
defense, however, I can cover both big and small men. I can also
bring the ball upcourt when our guards are being pressured."

Action!

Anthony's ability to do so many things well has made him a valuable player coming off the bench. His coach can watch a game develop and then send him in to take advantage of another team's weakness. In 1994–95, Anthony won the NBA's Sixth Man Award as the league's best non-starter.

Anthony says he is not a great leaper, but this play against Golden State's Chris Mullin shows he can jump high enough!

The referee and Coach Riley try to calm down Anthony after a brief scuffle during the 1995 NBA Finals.

nthony Mason thrives on body contact *and* eye contact. Both are important elements of his game. But it is his passion for winning that truly sets him apart. Anthony will not tolerate anything less than a total effort, from himself or from his teammates. Sometimes this causes tempers to flare, but not for long. His fellow Knicks know that he just wants to win.

nthony is not afraid to show his emotions—to his coach, to his teammates, or to opposing players.

 y most satisfying moment was when we beat the Chicago Bulls in the 1994 playoffs after they had us down by 17 points."

Anthony (left) has some fun with Chicago's Will Perdue as Horace Grant (#54) acts as peacekeeper.

Dealing

F lying elbows and physical play are a part of life in the NBA. Players must keep their cool, and the league punishes those who don't. The league also has a rule that any player on the court who is bleeding must leave immediately for treatment.

In a 1990 CBA game, Anthony caught an elbow in the mouth and lost a couple of teeth. How did he react?

"I knew it was an accident, but I was still very angry. I thought about retaliating, but that would have started a fight and gotten me thrown out of the game. And that would not have helped my team. So I decided to focus my emotions on something positive and took it out on the other team. I think I had scored six points when the incident occurred. By the time the final buzzer sounded, I had 42 points and 17 rebounds. I think teams were extra careful not to hit me with elbows after that!"

Anthony receives treatment for a cut lip.

With It

How Does

For someone with a big, strong build, like Anthony Mason, a good spin move can create all kinds of opportunities for you to score and problems for defenders trying to guard you. How can you develop this move? When a defender comes up close behind you, try to determine where they are putting their weight. If you feel an arm or body pushing on your right side, pivot on your right foot and spin to your left—that first step will place your body between the defender and the ball and open up a direct lane to the basket. If you feel someone on your left side, pivot on your left foot and spin to your right. The result will be the same . . . two points! or an assist for one of your teammates.

After spinning off his defenders, Anthony drives to the hoop.

He Do It?

The Grind

The life of an NBA player is not as glamorous as some people think. The constant travel is tiring. And it's hard to get a good night's sleep on a hotel bed when—like Anthony Mason—you are more than six-and-a-half feet tall!

"Being a professional athlete means learning how to deal with a lot of different people. I do not understand some of them, especially the ones who want to 'get in my face' because I am a famous basketball player. Of course, that just shows they do not understand me, either."

Anthony has a unique approach when it comes to "sending a message." He uses his head!

Anthony wears a message on his head as he signs a new contract before the start of the 1995–96 season.

Family

Anthony Mason lives in White Plains, New York, with his two sons, Anthony Jr. and Antoine. White Plains is a city of 55,000 people, 35 miles north of New York City. It takes him an hour to drive the 35 miles from his house to Madison Square Garden, where the Knicks play. During the season, he enjoys his huge video collection and watches as many movies as he can. During the summer, he takes trips with his family. Anthony's mother is still his biggest fan. She lives nearby in a home that he purchased for her after he signed his first big NBA contract. He also bought her season tickets, so he can see her at every Knicks home game!

Anthony brings his son Antoine to a press conference during the 1994 NBA Finals.

Matters

Say What?

What do basketball people say about Anthony Mason?

"When he gets riled up, he plays better and harder."

—*Pat Riley,*
   former New York Knicks coach

"He knows how to play!"

—*Larry Reid,*
   Tennessee State University coach

"He can rebound, run the court, and is a great passer."

—*Marty Blake, NBA scouting director*

"I don't think there's a big man in the league who can stay with him."

—*John Starks,*
  New York Knicks teammate

"When I saw him play in that first camp with us, I thought, 'What a steal!'"

—*Patrick Ewing,*
  New York Knicks teammate

Career

Anthony helped the Knicks come within one game of winning the NBA title in 1994. He scored 17 points and pulled down 9 rebounds to lead his team to victory in Game Five of the Finals.

In a college game against rival school East Tennessee, Anthony had to fill in at point guard for his team. Always up to the challenge, he got 10 assists, 28 points, and 10 rebounds.

Highlights

Anthony made a career-high 56.6 percent of his shots during the 1994–95 season. Only Chris Gatling, Horace Grant, and Shaquille O'Neal shot more accurately!

Anthony grabs a rebound from Houston's Hakeem Olajuwon.

lthough he has been New York's "super sub" since the 1991–92 season, Anthony had never won the NBA Sixth Man Award before the 1994–95 season (although he did finish in a second-place tie for the award in 1992–93).

Anthony dunks during Game Five of the 1994 NBA Finals against Houston.

nthony has averaged a rebound every four minutes during his NBA career—a better mark than his hero, Julius Erving, who averaged one every five minutes.

Reaching

Anthony Mason has millions of fans, and he loves them all. But a little boy named Joey will always have a special place in Anthony's heart. Joey was in New York's Mt. Sinai Hospital receiving treatment for leukemia, a very serious disease. His doctor got word to Anthony that one of his biggest fans was very ill and wanted to see him. Joey couldn't believe his eyes when Anthony Mason walked through the door with his arms full of Knicks souvenirs! Anthony sat with Joey until the boy was too weak to stay awake, then gave him an autographed photo and said goodbye.

The next morning, Joey died. Anthony dedicated the rest of the season to Joey's memory, and took the court each night wearing sneakers with Joey's name on them.

A few years ago, Anthony Mason and his teammates heard that the Boys Brotherhood Republic was in deep financial trouble. The community service center had been providing assistance and guidance to needy kids on New York's Lower

Out

Anthony signs an autograph for one of his many fans. Children have a special place in Anthony Mason's heart.

East Side for more than 60 years, but now money was about to run out. Anthony was one of several Knicks who donated clothing, money, and many hours of their time visiting and talking with underprivileged children. A few days before Christmas, Anthony volunteered to hand out baskets filled with food and toys. What a hit he was! For the children, it was like seeing the world's largest Santa Claus. For Mason, it was one of the most joyful moments of his life. He didn't even bother to wipe the tears from his eyes.

Numbers

Name: Anthony George Douglas Mason

Nickname: "Mase"

Born: December 14, 1966

Height: 6' 7"

Weight: 250 pounds

Uniform Number: 14

College: Tennessee State University

Anthony is 6' 7" tall . . . but he "plays bigger" because he is 7' 2" from fingertip to fingertip!

Season	Team	Games	Shooting Percentage	Free Throw Percentage	Assists Per Game	Rebounds Per Game	Points Per Game
1989-90	New Jersey Nets	21	35.0	60.0	0.3	1.6	1.8
1990-91	Denver Nuggets	3	50.0	75.0	0.0	1.7	3.3
1991-92	New York Knicks	82	50.9	64.2	1.3	7.0	7.0
1992-93	New York Knicks	81	50.2	68.2	2.1	7.9	10.3
1993-94	New York Knicks	73	47.6	72.1	2.1	5.8	7.2
1994-95	New York Knicks	77	56.6	64.1	3.1	8.4	9.9
1995-96	New York Knicks	82	56.3	72.0	4.4	9.3	14.6
Reg. Season Totals		419	52.6	68.1	2.5	7.4	9.4

What If...

I never doubted that I would make it in the pros—all I ever asked for in my life was an opportunity. But what if the Knicks had not given me that opportunity? Or what if I had been injured or become ill? Because I had studied criminal justice in school, there was another path I could follow. Today, I would probably be working as a police officer, federal agent, or lawyer—putting the bad guys in jail and keeping the good guys out. That is why it is so important to stay in school, play a sport, and join a boys' or girls' club. Believe in your dreams and never give up on anything. And if you need help, don't be afraid to ask for it."

Glossary

ACCURATE exact; correct

BRUTAL cruel; beastly

DEFICIT disadvantage; shortage

FINANCIAL concerning the management of money

SCHOLARSHIP money given to a student to help pay for schooling

UNIQUE singular; one of a kind

FUNCTION to perform a task

INCIDENT an event; an episode

LEGITIMATE legal; lawful

MASSIVE big and bulky

PRIOR before; earlier

RETALIATE repay; get back at; avenge

Index

About The Author

Mark Stewart grew up in New York City in the 1960s and 1970s—when the Mets, Jets, and Knicks all had championship teams. As a child, Mark read everything about sports he could lay his hands on. Today, he is one of the busiest sportswriters around. Since 1990, he has written close to 500 sports stories for kids, including profiles on more than 200 athletes, past and present. A graduate of Duke University, Mark served as senior editor of *Racquet*, a national tennis magazine, and was managing editor of *Super News*, a sporting goods industry newspaper. He is the author of every Grolier All-Pro Biography.